FAMILY PETS

OUR PET RABBIT

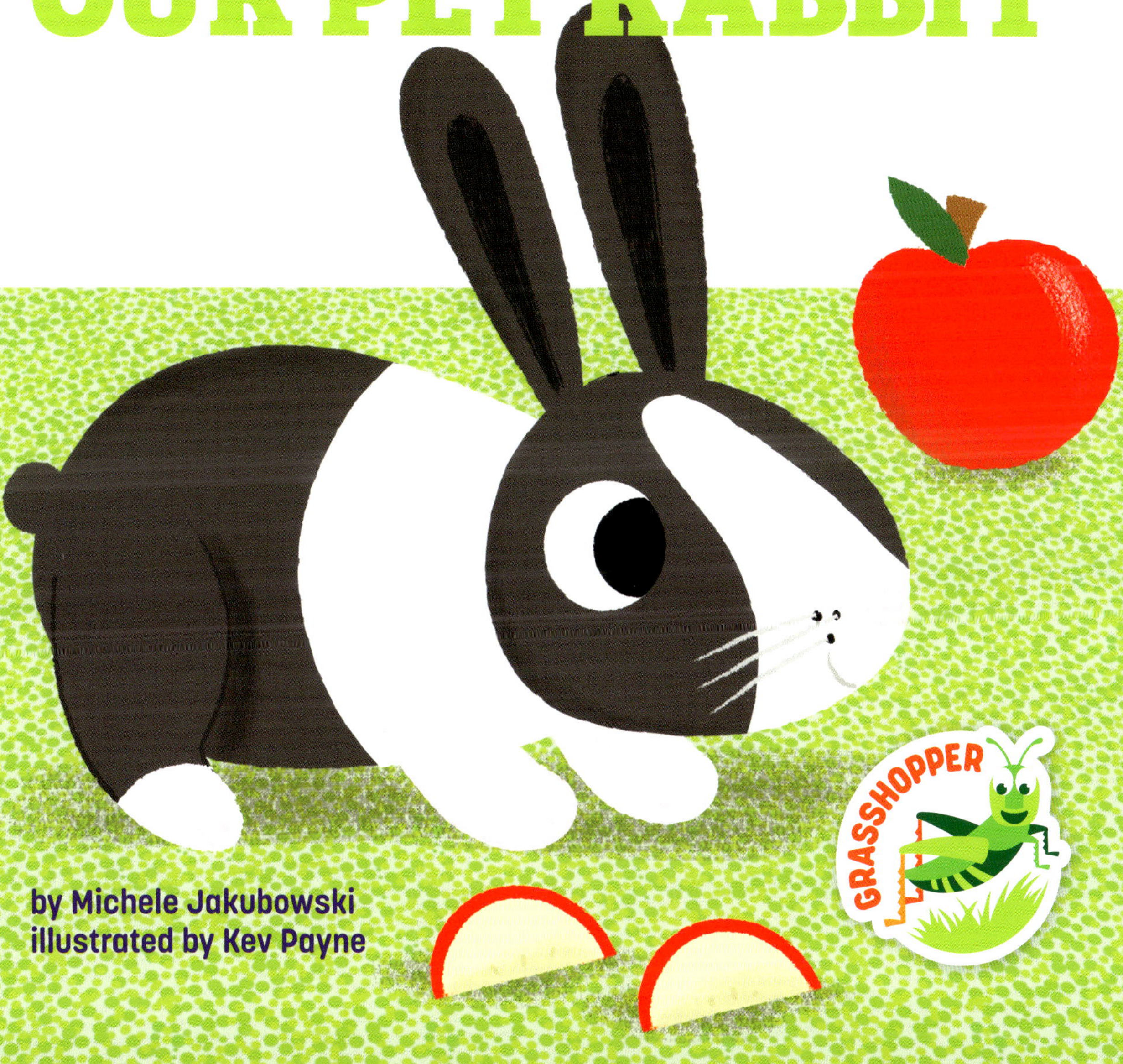

by Michele Jakubowski
illustrated by Kev Payne

GRASSHOPPER

Tools for Parents & Teachers

Grasshopper Books enhance imagination and introduce the earliest readers to fiction with fun storylines and illustrations. The easy-to-read text supports early reading experiences with repetitive sentence patterns and sight words.

Before Reading

- Look at the cover illustration. What do readers see? What do they think the book will be about?
- Look at the picture glossary together. Sound out the words. Ask readers to identify the first letter of each vocabulary word.

Read the Book

- "Walk" through the book, reading to or along with the reader. Point to the illustrations as you read.

After Reading

- Review the picture glossary again. Ask readers to locate the words in the text.
- Ask the reader: Callie and Liam build a castle for their pet rabbit, Bella. If you had a pet rabbit, what would you build for it?

Grasshopper Books are published by Jump!
5357 Penn Avenue South
Minneapolis, MN 55419
www.jumplibrary.com

Library of Congress Cataloging-in-Publication Data

Names: Jakubowski, Michele, author.
Payne, Kev, 1978- illustrator.
Title: Our pet rabbit / by Michele Jakubowski
illustrated by Kev Payne.
Description: Minneapolis, MN: Jump!, Inc., [2022]
Series: Family pets
Includes reading tips and supplementary back matter.
Audience: Ages 5-7.
Identifiers: LCCN 2020058539 (print)
LCCN 2020058540 (ebook)
ISBN 9781636902050 (paperback)
ISBN 9781636902043 (hardcover)
ISBN 9781636902067 (ebook)
Subjects: LCSH: Readers (Primary)
Rabbits–Juvenile fiction.
Classification: LCC PE1119.2 .J355 2022 (print)
LCC PE1119.2 (ebook)
DDC 428.6/2–dc23
LC record available at https://lccn.loc.gov/2020058539
LC ebook record available at https://lccn.loc.gov/2020058540

Editor: Eliza Leahy
Direction and Layout: Anna Peterson
Illustrator: Kev Payne

Printed in the United States of America at Corporate Graphics in North Mankato, Minnesota.

Table of Contents

Bella's Castle

This is our pet rabbit, Bella.

She likes to play in boxes.

My brother, Liam, stacks boxes.

I cut cardboard.

We are making
a castle for Bella!

“Do you like it, Bella?” I ask.

Bella hops away.
She chews on her toy.

“I don’t think she likes it, Callie,” Liam says.

"Maybe she's hungry," I say.

I give Bella fresh hay.

Liam puts pellets in her bowl.

Bella hops away.

"Maybe she wants fresh water," Liam says.

I fill her water bowl.

Liam cleans her litter box.

Bella hops away.

“Where did Bella go?” I ask.

“I don’t know!” says Liam.

We look under the couch.
We look behind the chair.

“She’s in the castle!” says Liam.

"High five, Bella!"
says Liam.

He holds out his hand.
Bella high-fives.

I give her an apple slice.
"Good job, Bella!" I say.

Let's Review!

What treat does Callie give Bella?

A. a carrot **B.** a cupcake **C.** an apple slice **D.** a banana

Picture Glossary

cardboard
Thick, stiff paper used for making boxes and other things.

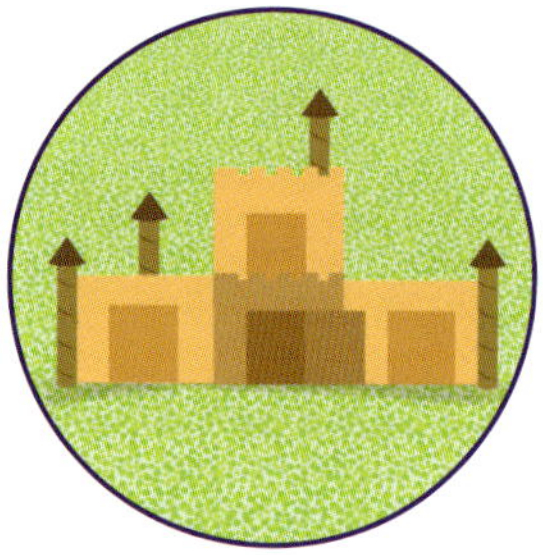

castle
A large building with high walls and towers that is built to protect against attack.

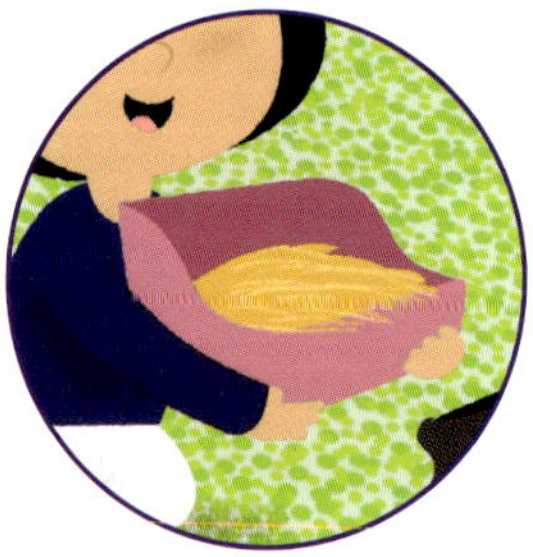

litter box
A place rabbits use as a toilet.

pellets
Small, hard pieces of food.

Let's Review! Answer Key: C. an apple slice